MARRIED to the DREAM

MARRIED to the DREAM

AN IVF JOURNEY

Ericka Michelle Richburg · With C. NaTasha Richburg

MARRIED TO THE DREAM:
An IVF Journey

Published by Gatekeeper Press
7853 Gunn Hwy., Suite 209
Tampa, FL 33626
www.GatekeeperPress.com

ISBN (paperback): 9781662939143
eISBN: 9781662939150

Contents

Introduction   1

1. New Dawn   3

2. Ericka's Backstory   5

3. Counseling   9

4. IVF for a Second Time as a Single Parent   15

5. Secondary Infertility   19

6. The Stitch Is Doing the Babysitting   25

7. Labor and Delivery at Twenty-Seven Weeks   31

8. Finding My Village   35

9. It Is All About Perspective   37

10. A Smile Burns Sunlight Through Every Dark Cloud   41

11. The Aha Moment   43

Introduction

The decision to have two IVF babies meant that even after her divorce, Ericka remained "Married to the Dream" that she would get pregnant via in vitro fertilization (IVF) for a second time. The Dream afforded the mother of one a sibling for her first IVF baby. She had to accept that single parenthood was a viable way of life until a future, committed, loving relationship with a caring, devoted partner happened. The Dream of having two IVF babies moved into overdrive and pushed away the stereotype that she needed a husband to support her decision to have a second child. The Dream would bring all who are meant to be in her space to become a part of Ericka's future.

Learning to be grateful and reside in life's happy place, Ericka authors this book to share the path she used to reach the joy of parenthood. Ericka hopes that others will learn from her IVF experiences. Her mom wants others to understand the importance of supporting another's Dream. We realize that this is one of many paths. However, Ericka's path is one path with many turns and twists. She provides unique advice associated with the nuances of infertility.

Ericka is grateful for the family and friends who stayed around to bear witness to her celebratory times. One friend, in particular, has provided a listening ear, encouraging words, and a consistent presence. That friend has done a lot to support Ericka on this journey. He has provided meaningful affirmations in the dark and added shine to her light. Ericka, in turn, has also had the opportunity to encourage her friends. She is an excellent card giver and always remembers a holiday or chance to give a meaningful gift. Ericka knows that infertility can be a complex subject for some people to discuss. She speaks openly about her journey to help increase the understanding of those beginning their IVF journey. She is here for you. Feel free to contact her at thecnrproductions2@gmail.com. For the family members who don't know what to say or how to approach the subject, don't hesitate to contact Ericka's mother, C. NaTasha, at thecnrproductions@gmail.com. We are a team prepared to share our journey as both the person going through IVF and the person supporting them along the way.

1. New Dawn

by C. NaTasha Richburg

Impatient

Patient

Resistance

Resolved

Destined for victory

Problems now solved

The foresight of questions once asked

Progressed fast

A mother's babies are born

Life's Dream embraces a new dawn

2. Ericka's Backstory

by Ericka Michelle

Growing up, wanting to become a mother included the idea that a husband would be foremost in the process. In my mind, he would love, cherish, respect, and honor me. He would treat me like a queen. We would meet and marry and start our family on our honeymoon night. Nine months later, I would become the mother of my firstborn child. I would nurture my child. The warm, sweet scent of my loving mother aura that only a doting husband can inhale fills the room. The space of our collective breath creates an embrace with reciprocal motions like solar energy. His sun intertwines with my sun. We are both beams of life's illuminations. We shower our child with hugs and kisses that ride on the sunbeams of our collective smiles. We would laugh and have great times together. That was the story in my head.

Outside my head, my life did not carry as many sunlit visions as I once imagined. Yet, I remained Married to the Dream. The Dream was that I would be a mother. I remember what my mother would always say in response to me not being a mother, "You are not a mother . . . YET! Always remember 'yet' along with the phase of not being a mother."

Not fully understanding the importance of the word "yet," I now overstand that the word "yet" carried my Dream of becoming a mother.

Before I truly understood the premise of "yet," I carried the shame of being unable to affirm and address fertility questions. The stares from people wanting to know when I would have a baby. Why had I not had a positive pregnancy test after various fertility attempts? The question put me in the stance to block, duck, and hide from my unwanted offenses that overshadowed the possibility of happiness. Putting on weight was an offensive move that steered the conversation to let me hide my infertility. After ten years of unhappiness in a marriage, I divorced him. The word "yet" lingered as I remained "Married to the Dream" of becoming a mother.

I moved on to jump into the abyss with an unfriendly attribute disguised as a second husband who verbally discarded me at the pronouncement of my positive pregnancy news. He did not celebrate the notion that it took 4,718 days for me to get pregnant. I divorced him. Remaining "Married to the Dream," I gave birth to my firstborn child the day before my divorce was made final. I met and dated several people after the birth of my daughter. Only one man became my lifelong friend. He also became a willing participant who availed himself to support my Dream. Though not the father of my children, he is a constant reminder of the attributes of a loving, committed partner. I always remained "Married to my Dream." My friend also attached his kind-hearted behavior to my Dream. I appreciate him for doing so.

My life's Dream has resulted in three foundational lessons. First, I remained "Married to the Dream" of having a family with several children of whom I gave birth. Second, I learned a smile would burn its sunlight through every dark cloud. Third, the foundation of a significant and lasting friendship brings peaceful-calm waters during life's most challenging times. That is the Dream I am married to for now and forever more. Finding peace in life's turbulent waters was a result of counseling. My counselor helped me understand life and what I could do differently. The next chapter gives a glimpse of my experience with counseling.

3. Counseling

by C. NaTasha Richburg

Our world affords dreams, visions, hopes, and aspirational pursuits to all who are willing to imagine success beyond our circumstances. Many of us hope that a loved one will love us as it happens on TV. This storybook expectation can result in a dark turn of events that may hurt our feelings. Sometimes the change breaks our hearts. The difference can make us seek clarification about our role in the relationship. When life turns negative, we may feel off-balance while walking on solid ground. As we imagine, the concrete foundation of life in our daily walk feels typically safe. However, the confusing world around us starts to spin. We wonder, *Is it me? Did I do something to make them mad? I know I did something wrong to get the silent treatment.* These are thoughts that make us question life.

Ericka's world spiraled downward after being informed by her husband that he did not want her or her unborn child after waiting 4,718 days to get pregnant. That negative comment led her onto the road to counseling. This chapter is presented in the format of the interviewer. I ask questions so Ericka can offer insight into her counseling experience.

Before we get started, as a person witnessing Ericka's counseling journey, I know that counseling helped Ericka get in touch with her emotions and find all that is good about what resonates within her psyche. I watched Ericka heal from a horrific experience with a person to whom she was legally bound. Read that story in her book, *Abandoned Guilt and Absorbed Gladness*, to learn the details of Ericka's journey.

Ericka, in your own words, explain why you believe counseling helped during the IVF process when you felt off-kilter and out of sync.

Counseling is essential because it allows me to express myself in a non-biased manner. The person listening gives me the tools and advice to help me cope with what I'm experiencing. The counselor lets me know I have someone to talk to about life. A counselor is someone who listens without judgment.

According to www.counseling.org:

> *Counseling is **a collaborative effort between the counselor and the client**. Professional counselors help clients identify goals and potential solutions to problems that cause emotional turmoil; seek to improve communication and coping skills; strengthen self-esteem; and promote behavior change and optimal mental health.*

What did you learn from your counseling experience?
I learned from the counseling experience that I only know some things. Now I understand that life is a continuous learning opportunity. I also discovered that although I have excellent qualities, I have flaws. My flaws only sometimes work in my favor. So, through counseling, I know how to navigate them.

Counseling allows what works best to shine through to help me become a better decision-maker. For example, my choice of men came from how I viewed myself. I realized that if I had a higher view of myself, those choices would have never happened, had I learned through the counseling experience earlier.

What is social counseling?

Social counseling is a support group or group therapy. You are with people going through similar things and phases of life. In the group setting, we learn from one another with the guidance of a professional.

According to: Socialworklicensure.org

Counselors typically focus on helping families and individuals with specific problems, particularly patients with mental health disorders. On the other hand, social workers focus on providing a more comprehensive range of services in social service systems.

What is genetic counseling?

Since I used anonymous sperm for my second child, I participated in genetic counseling. Genetic counseling is when you sit before a genetic specialist, and they go over male and female biology. So, they talk about you and the anonymous donor's genetic makeup and see if you are a match. If you have issues in different areas, the counselor will point them out. That way, you make an informed decision about your future embryo.

According to The National Society of Genetic Counselors :

- *Genetic counselors are an essential part of your healthcare team.*

- *Genetic counselors have advanced training in medical genetics. They guide and support patients seeking more information about how inherited diseases and conditions might affect them or their families and interpret genetic test results based on their personal and family history.*

- *Genetic counselors can meet with individuals or families before or after genetic testing.*

- *Genetic counselors are specialized in prenatal, pediatric, oncology, neurology, ophthalmology, psychiatry, and many other areas.*

- *Many genetic counselors can see patients via telehealth options.*

- *In addition to different specialty areas, genetic counselors can have roles outside of seeing patients. Genetic counselors can work in research, education, industry, marketing, and many other parts across the healthcare and genetics fields.*

Are married couples and single parents expected to participate in counseling?

Couples may sometimes attend social work counseling as it relates to IVF. In that case, that is when you meet with a social worker. The social worker's role is to tell you diverse ways to have an age-appropriate conversation with your child or children as they age. The social worker also prepares clients to be single parents. For example, children may want to know the reason that they don't have a father or mother. The counselor will give you the tools to stand firm in your decision to be a single parent. You learn to celebrate the "choice" of being a single parent, showing your child the positive light of having a mommy or daddy who wanted them. Social workers help families of any type to celebrate their uniqueness, embrace it, and feel unashamed.

How often should married couples go to counseling?

According to: Apeacefullifecounseling.com on February 1, 2016, *by*
KAT MINDENHALL, LCSW

Kat Mindenhall recommends weekly sessions for the first 4-6 weeks and then re-evaluate afterward. That isn't a requirement, but there are several good reasons to consider doing this when you are wondering how often you should come to couples counseling:

- *You want your couple's therapist to get through the assessment period quickly.*

- *You want to get the most out of the momentum of being new and fresh in therapy.*

- *Coming in less frequently means you are starting over each time.*

- *Gains are more profound and powerful when they can immediately follow from a previous experience.*

- *You'll be able to accurately determine whether to step down to twice a month with a perspective on how it feels to have more frequent visits.*

- *It makes you vulnerable to dropping out prematurely or adds sessions to the overall number you attend.*

Being single does not mean, as a parent, you are alone. Being married doesn't mean the parents act as a team. Each primary caregiver may feel alone. A community of people is needed to help guide someone through IVF and the birthing process. You can go right if you include counseling as part of the community needed to support you in the IVF process.

4. IVF for a Second Time as a Single Parent

by C. NaTasha Richburg

This book ventures outside the scope of Ericka's first book to address the changes in the rules of IVF. The new rules benefit single women's access to the IVF process without the benefit of marriage. The day after her first baby's birth, her divorce was final. She was officially a single parent at age thirty-four. She joined the dating scene hoping to meet her life's partner. However, with her biological clock still ticking, the urgency to conceive again beat loud with reminders about the challenges of producing healthy eggs beyond age thirty-five. The loud beat did not dim her hope of having a sibling for her daughter.

She took vitamins described in Rebecca Fett's 2014 book, *It Starts with the Egg: How the Science of Egg Quality Can Help You Get Pregnant Naturally, Prevent Miscarriage, and Improve Your Odds in IVF*. There was a remarkable increase in egg production as follows:

First baby IVF Retrieval cycle	Second baby IVF Retrieval cycle
36 eggs retrieved	55 eggs retrieved
28 matured	29 matured
4 embryos	11 embryos
2 normal embryos	5 normal embryos
1 embryo was used (Baby girl)	1 embryo was used (Baby boy)
1 discarded	4 embryos (3 passed testing and were donated)
	18 eggs (frozen and saved)

The nurse teased Ericka that as she got older, her eggs got younger. Of course, that is not true. However, her egg retrieval success rate increased from 36 to 55 eggs, approximately 53%. Facing the challenges of going through IVF again, Ericka endured comments from people who didn't understand her calling to be a mother. Those voices sizzled and evaporated into the sky, never to resonate with meaning in her desire to fulfill her calling to become a mother of multiple children.

There is good news for single women. Beginning January 1, 2021, Maryland began offering unwed women IVF insurance coverage. The details of that decision are summarized in www.shadygrove-fertility.com article dated February 23, 2021: "Maryland Mandate Opens New Door for Single Mothers by Choice." Ericka became a single mother of two "by choice" because she wanted her baby to have a sibling. With 24/7 family support, everyone in her family's household agrees with and supports this decision.

Ericka prepared for her new round of IVF and the scrutiny she would endure as a single woman. Initially, she was caught off guard by this new level of IVF protocol oversight about her anonymous sperm. That oversight would have been welcome in her unhappy marriage with an unsupportive husband. There are necessary checks and rechecks on the background of the sperm bank's donor sperm. Ericka had to accept the donor sperm oversight experience as a crucial aspect of the IVF protocol process, which made her acutely aware of the attributes of single parenthood.

There are no guarantees in the IVF process, just the chance to walk down every open path on Hope's Road until all potential remedies are exhausted. Ericka began her journey at twenty and gave herself until forty to engage her IVF path to motherhood. Every person is different. Every path has other peaks and valleys. Regardless of the path, we all can embrace the audacity to hope. We can hope for a brighter tomorrow. We all can live in the hope that our Dream of IVF parenthood is realized.

There are occasions when the conception of the first child goes off without a hitch. However, after a year or two of trying, one may need an examination to determine if they are experiencing secondary infertility.

5. Secondary Infertility

by C. NaTasha & Ericka Michelle

Many have come before you and have had successful pregnancies. This chapter will let you know what I learned on my IVF journey. Some couples struggle with conception when trying to conceive a baby for a second time after a successful natural birth. The thought that since the pregnancy was relatively easy, the second time would be the same as the first may cause concern. Concern can take the form of shame, thinking work stresses and life strains result in deep trouble with conception. The pain associated with infertility challenges the expectation that giving birth is an effortless process. The hurt of infertility is exacerbated by the inquiries exposed by family members, who wonder, "When are you giving your child a sibling? They need someone to play with. You don't want them to be alone . . . do you?"

The bubble of joyous anticipation covered anguish when six months passed, nine months passed, twelve months passed—and no positive pregnancy test. You think, *this didn't happen with my first pregnancy*. The thoughts ring loudly in the head of the couples trying to conceive again. *What's next? What do we need to do?* First, they must empower themselves with knowledge about what it means to carry a second pregnancy after a natural birth.

According to CDC FastStats accessed December 5, 2022, www.cdc.gov/nchs/fastats/infertility.htm, 12.2% percent of women ages 15-49 used infertility services. Second, make an appointment with your doctor to check this out. Read about secondary infertility to ask informed questions during your doctor's visit.

According to <u>the Cleveland Clinic</u> :
Secondary infertility is the inability to conceive a child or carry a pregnancy to full term after previously giving birth. Classifying one as having secondary infertility means they had a previous successful birth that did not require fertility medications or treatments, like in vitro fertilization. Secondary infertility is typically diagnosed after unsuccessfully conceiving for six months to a year. A related condition is recurrent pregnancy loss, where patients and couples can conceive but cannot carry to term. [Cleveland Clinic website, Accessed March 20, 2023, <u>https://my.clevelandclinic.org/health/diseases/21139-secondary-infertility</u>]

What are the causes of secondary infertility in women?
Causes of secondary infertility in women include:

- ***Problems in the quantity or quality of eggs:*** *Women are born with a limited supply of eggs and need help to create new eggs after birth. As women approach their forties and beyond, the numbers of eggs left in their ovaries decrease, and the remaining eggs have a higher chance of having chromosomal problems. For women whose age isn't a concern, there are other reasons they might have a low number of good-quality eggs, including autoimmune or genetic conditions and prior surgery or radiation.*

- ***Problems with the fallopian tubes:*** *The fallopian tubes carrying eggs from the ovaries to the uterus can become blocked due to pelvic infections such as chlamydia or gonorrhea.*

- ***Problems with the uterus:*** *Many conditions related to the uterus can cause secondary infertility. Scarring can occur during a dilation and curettage (D&C) or Cesarean delivery, creating uterine adhesions that interfere with future pregnancies. Fibroids or polyps are benign (non-cancerous) growths inside the uterus that can impair pregnancy. A retained placenta can cause infection and uterine scarring.*

- ***Endometriosis*** *is a condition where tissue that usually grows inside the uterus grows elsewhere in the body, such as on the ovaries or bowel surfaces. While endometriosis is common, not all endometriosis causes infertility.*

- ***Polycystic ovary syndrome*** *is a hormonal disorder characterized by longer-than-normal or infrequent menstrual periods. Women with this condition have excessive male hormones, and the ovaries fail to release eggs regularly.*

- ***Breastfeeding:*** *If a woman feeds her baby only by breastfeeding, her body stops ovulating or releasing eggs for potential fertilization.*

- ***Weight gain or other lifestyle changes:*** *Weight gain can lead to ovary dysfunction in some patients. Specific diets may affect fertility. Medications may also affect fertility.*

Causes of secondary infertility in men include:

Reduced testosterone level

Testosterone plays a crucial role in sperm production. Testosterone levels can decline due to aging, injury to urinary or genital organs, or certain medical conditions. These conditions include:

- *Genital infections*
- *Thyroid diseases*
- *Diabetes*
- *Tuberculosis*
- *Mumps*
- *Smallpox*
- *Blood diseases*
- *Benign tumors*
- *Emotional stress*
- *Myocardial infarction*
- *Coma*
- *Stroke*
- *Respiratory failure*
- *Congestive heart failure*
- *Burns*
- *Sepsis is a potentially life-threatening reaction to infection.*
- *Surgery in the genital tract*
- *The presence of myco-plasma, which is a type of bacteria*
- *Anesthesia*

[Cleveland Clinic website. , Accessed March 20, 2023, https://my.clevelandclinic.org/health/diseases/21139-secondary-infertility]

Know that you are not alone on this journey. I have met people along the way who had one successful pregnancy and won't seek help to evaluate why they haven't been able to get pregnant a second time. If that's you, please don't age out the fertility-age range without investigating why you have not conceived. What does it hurt? So, you may not like the doctor's answer.

What happens if the doctor offers you an approach that will ensure a successful pregnancy? That is what happened for me. My doctor explored my reproductive organs and determined my fallopian tubes were leaking, which he summarized as the primary cause of my infertility. Once my fallopian tubes were removed, my body was prime to proceed successfully through the IVF process. Just have a fertility specialist examine you. You may learn something that can help you conceive.

With a successful embryo transfer for my second baby, I was on my way to ensuring a sibling for my daughter. I had bleeding. Because I had bleeding with my first child, I wasn't worried but went to the emergency room to check everything. All was well. However, when I visited my doctor, I learned about the seriousness of my growing pregnancy.

6. The Stitch Is Doing the Babysitting

by C. NaTasha Richburg

In the season of seeking encouraging words, I listened to a sermon by Dr. John Maxwell entitled, "Every Miracle Starts with a Problem." We all have problems and sometimes think of issues in only one dimension and may feel inadequate. There is a positive opportunity to think of a situation differently. A problem can represent a push, a driver, or a turn signal that forges a new direction for our life. The problem that drove Ericka's miracle was the 4,718 days it took to achieve a positive pregnancy test. The miracle that resulted in pursuing the problem in Ericka's life was resolved. Yes, the birth of her daughter, now two years old, fixed her infertility problem. Now, this phase of motherhood continues with Ericka's second IVF pregnancy. With the new level of complications with a pregnancy, using the voice of the streets, "the sh&# is getting real." Women's aging results in a new level of precautions necessary to forge through a successful pregnancy.

The best outcome of getting older and reaching age thirty-five is the close monitoring provided by maternal-fetal medicine doctors. Accordingly, the society of Maternal-Fetal Medicine's website https://www.smfm.org/whatwedo, information retrieved on April 5, 2023.

Maternal-fetal medicine (MFM) subspecialists treat two patients at the same time. We partner with the mom-to-be, her family, and her medical team to navigate the un-routine and achieve the best possible outcome. [They] see families who have experienced high-risk pregnancies in the past, women with chronic health conditions, and women who develop unexpected problems during their pregnancy.

The very kind and capable maternal-fetal medicine doctors closely monitored Ericka's medical plan before the execution of her second IVF pregnancy. In other words, the doctors consulted Ericka at the very beginning with a planned approach for her pregnancy before the medical requirements of the IVF process began. All factors, such as preeclampsia in Ericka's first pregnancy and her age, were considered before IVF started. According to information retrieved on November 25, 2022, from Preeclampsia.org,

Preeclampsia is a severe pregnancy condition and can be particularly dangerous because many signs are silent, while some symptoms resemble "normal" effects of pregnancy on your body. Many women suffering from preeclampsia don't feel sick and may be surprised or frustrated when admitted to the hospital or prescribed bed rest since they still feel well.

In concert with Ericka's monthly OB-GYN appointments, she met with the maternal-fetal medicine doctors for extensive examinations twice a week as needed. On several occasions, the maternal-fetal medicine offices on the hospital campus afforded Ericka immediate access to hospital resources.

For example, at twenty weeks, Ericka was sent by the maternal-fetal medicine doctor to go to the Labor and Delivery (L &D) department for an extensive internal examination. The doctors determined that her cervix was beginning to open. On her twenty-second week visit, the maternal-fetal medicine doctor sent Ericka to L&D a second time to complete an extensive internal examination. At that time, the doctor's correct inclination was that Ericka needed a cervical cerclage to support carrying her baby to full term. According to information retrieved on November 25, 2022, from clevelandclinic.org :

Cervical cerclage keeps your cervix closed during pregnancy to prevent premature birth due to an incompetent (weakened) cervix. Your healthcare provider will likely recommend a cervical cerclage if your cervix has weakened. The procedure is to keep the fetus safe inside your uterus until it's time for you to give birth.

During this procedure, your healthcare provider will place one or several sutures (stitches) in the opening of your cervix to keep it safely closed during your pregnancy.

Your cervix is the lower portion or opening of your uterus. Your uterus is like a pouch or purse, and a cervical cerclage procedure is like strings that keep the purse closed.

Ericka went to the hospital, where her doctor's office is located, to stay overnight in the Labor and Delivery Unit for the cervical cerclage procedure the following day. With her two-year-old daughter at home, it caused a change in her daughter's bedtime ritual for one night, but the bedtime change was worth it. Her daughter and I FaceTimed with Ericka to involve her in all the goings-on in the house. We made the best of the circumstances. The IVF process is sometimes challenging; we have learned to roll with the punches.

Early Saturday morning, the doctors began the procedure. They used two stitches to stop the cervix from opening prematurely. Ericka's father and I did everything possible to support her at home. Ericka was allowed to leave the hospital once the numbness left her legs. By 5:00 p.m. on Saturday, Ericka was released from the hospital with an appointment scheduled for a follow-up the following Friday morning, which happened to be Veterans Day. I was off work so I attended the appointment with Ericka.

Upon completing the examination, good news filled the air. The enjoyment in the examination room was infectious, with a new sense of cautious hope that the pregnancy would progress as planned to a full-term delivery. The nurse gleefully exclaimed, "Now the stitches will do the babysitting." We hugged, relishing how the stitches provided the cervix a firm hold, giving the baby security to grow and be healthy.

I worried and prayed that Ericka would continue to be an African American success story with this pregnancy. There are many documented studies about African American women's lower pregnancy rates. For example, *Shady Grove Fertility* wrote in the article "ASRM 2018: SGF Examines Why African American Women Experience Lower Pregnancy Rates Associated with IVF as Compared with Caucasian Women," dated October 24, 2018:

> *"Our results suggest that African American women respond just as well to medications that stimulate egg production, produce as many eggs, and produce more good quality embryos than Caucasian patients," says Dr. Isaac E. Sasson, SGF physician and a key researcher on this study. "However, overall chances of success are decreased among African American patients. The total of these data suggest that uterine factors are the most likely cause of decreased success from IVF among African American patients," adds Sasson.*

Consistent with prior studies, this study found that birth rates per embryo transfer were 14 percent lower for African American women compared with Caucasian women as a result of both lower pregnancy rates and higher pregnancy losses.

"The good news is that armed with this information, African American women and their physicians can make more informed decisions about their gynecologic and fertility care. Preventive care can help detect potential problems in their earliest, easiest-to-treat state. Annual OB/GYN annual examinations are critical, as is seeking care early when a woman experiences infertility or recurrent miscarriage. Early treatment leads to much more favorable outcomes," adds Sasson.

"Unfortunately, in addition to lower live birth rates from IVF, African Americans are more likely to experience preterm birth following IVF, and uterine factors are most likely the cause. Fibroids disproportionately affect our African American population and likely contribute to the poorer outcomes observed in these two studies. The good news is that armed with this information, we can act as advocates for this patient population and do more research to further evaluate for causes and solutions," says Dr. Sasson, who was also a key researcher on this second study.

The bright light is that Ericka is happy to believe that all will be well. God is good. Ericka's support system, along with family and friends, are the people in her human resource office that support her quest to work at home if she is mandated to bed rest. A pregnancy under any circumstance may be difficult. Having an IVF pregnancy brings on occasions that require a knowledgeable team of doctors to manage the women's health care. Ericka's OB-GYN and maternal-fetal medical team provided the detailed care needed for carrying a healthy baby.

All the doctors working together didn't make Ericka's diagnosis better. Moving slowly to the thirty-seven-week delivery date took time and appeared impossible at times.

7. Labor and Delivery at Twenty-Seven Weeks

by Ericka Michelle

Sitting in the Labor and Delivery (L&D) room of the hospital at twenty-seven weeks and three days pregnant, the constant beeps of the machinery remind me of the dire constraints put upon me because something is off with my baby boy Erick-Julius. I went to the hospital because of swelling in my vagina; I thought the simple remedy would result in a prescription for an ointment or medicine that would allow me quick release from the emergency room. Not true!!

The doctors performing the routine examination were concerned about my baby boy's erratic heartbeat. I thought I would have a short in-and-out doctor's visit. However, the emergency room visit resulted in a nine-day stay with one-hundred percent bed rest. God had me go to the hospital's L&D department to receive the prenatal attention I would not have gotten otherwise.

My L&D stay created stressful uncertainty, but the staff made the stressful time positive. Everyone was kind and shared loving affection. The doctors and nurses were on top of my care. The medical staff would enter my room to get their daily dose of positivity and light. I was the gleeful talk of the nurses' station, which is a good thing because sometimes patients are the talk of the nurses' station incorrectly. I thanked them each day for taking great care of me to ensure Erick-Julius thrived and remained in my uterus until he got bigger and stronger!

My baby boy decided to make himself known to the nursing staff and doctors as he continued to baffle us about what to do with his prenatal care. I was strategically prompted and prepared by the doctors for a potential premature delivery. Behind the smile of my well-mannered behavior was my nervousness that wrapped my uneasiness in a big hug. The big hug calmed the nerves of those who presented me with the essence of their restless spirit. In other words, I was strategically set for premature delivery. It turned out that the swelling I experienced, which brought me to the emergency room in the first place, was the least of my worries.

My clothes were no longer streetwear. Now I was wearing hospital gowns that are open in the back. The gown exposed my backend to a shifting wind, a cold wind, to the stares of onlookers (only joking). The concept of a perfect pregnancy has emerged on the street, saying, "the s#!t is getting real." Though the situation was dangerous, I stayed calm and followed the doctor's orders. I loved how wonderful the nurses treated me.

My second IVF baby wanted to come into the world solely based on his terms. My first IVF baby, Miss Erielle, was on FaceTime saying, "Hi, Mommy." My mother and father stayed in a ready position to work as a team to support me in any way possible. My special friend, though not Erick-Julius's father, continuously offered kind words and hope for a perfect birth of my baby boy. The space of the L&D department of the hospital was the place where I found my village. They gave me good memories of gifted hands working together to benefit my healthy pregnancy and birth. I am so grateful for each of them.

God's plan for my pregnancy with my baby boy, Erick-Julius:

- June 23 embryo transfer

- July 5 blood pregnancy test (positive)

- July 7th second blood pregnancy test to make sure numbers increase

- July 15 (5th-week 6-days) heavy bleeding for the first time in the hospital

- July 28 (7th-week 5-days) heavy bleeding for a second time in hospital

- October 22, (20th-week 6-days), short cervix began progesterone suppositories

  According to the article, "Cervical length: Why does it matter during pregnancy?" Mayo Clinic Retrieved April 5, 2023, Answer From Yvonne Butler Tobah, M.D., states in part, the *cervical length refers to the length of the lower end of the uterus. During pregnancy, the length of the cervix might shorten too soon, increasing the risk of preterm labor and premature birth. Preterm labor is labor that begins between 20 weeks and 36 weeks and 6 days of pregnancy. The earlier premature birth happens, the greater the health risks for the baby.*

- November 5 (22nd-week) cerclage (stitch is doing the babysitting)

  According to the American Pregnancy Association website https://americanpregnancy.org/healthy-pregnancy/

pregnancy-complications/cervical-cerclage/accessed on April 5, 2023, *Treatment for cervical incompetence is a surgical procedure called cervical cerclage, also known as cerclage, in which the cervix is sewn closed during pregnancy. The cervix is the lowest part of the uterus and extends into the vagina.*

- November 11 saw the cerclage gave an extra two cm

- December 13 (27th-week 3-days) admitted to hospital due to the baby's heart rate dips

- January 27 (33 weeks 6-days), emergency C-section, we welcomed my son

- February 10, the baby leaves the Neonatal Intensive Care Unit (NICU) to go home and meet his sister

8. Finding My Village

by Ericka Michelle

A reflection on when I was admitted to the Labor and Delivery (L&D) room under the constant hum of medical instruments: The musical notes loom mainly in a fusion-jazz progression. The melody is soothing due to the peaks and valleys of the sounds, letting us know that all is well. Suddenly, only one note comes through the medical equipment as doctors and nurses rush into the room, only to notice the fetal monitor has dropped on my stomach. The doctors no longer could hear the baby's heartbeat. The doctors and nurses are grateful that I, as their patient, will be as pleased as they are, and mutual bonding ensues. They become a village of medical workers offering well wishes and optimism in a high-tension situation.

Nine days straight in the hospital on bed rest was not "rest" in the traditional sense of being. It was a captured state of observation and measurements. Rest was not the outcome of my days and nights. It was nerve-racking. I felt like a prisoner of sorts. My only crime was trying to allow my baby to grow inside me before his entry into the world happened. It started at twenty-two weeks, and now I was at week twenty-nine, motivated to make it to week thirty-two before I was commanded to go to the operating room for my C-Section.

The hospital's team of doctors and nurses listened to my IVF story. They encouraged me. They heard me. Finally, I have a village of well-wishers. Individuals pop into my room to share their stories. We had many common paths in life. I felt their hearts. I felt the heart of the village. After many years of friendship disappointment, I finally found a village of good-hearted people.

I got up from bed rest to attend my baby shower. Though the doctors were displeased by my decision, they wanted to see the photos of my baby shower. The baby shower brought me joy. The doctors and nurses also brought me joy when they shared my happy images. I learned many lessons, which start with following your heart. My heart said that going to a happy baby shower would make me feel better if my baby did not get worse. I felt joy when the entire staff wanted to look at my pictures that could not be assessed with a price. The gratitude I felt from being in their company made me feel like I had found my village.

In addition to my healthcare village, a longtime friend who happens to be a mother of three beautiful children has reentered my life as a daily reminder of what having a best friend means. We have a girl talk. We laugh a lot. My BFF has shown me what it's like to be spontaneous by attending unplanned lunch dates. She is a light. She is a joy. She makes my life feel full.

> **"You are not the product of your mistakes but the lessons you embrace."**
>
> —Ericka Michelle

9. LESSONS LEARNED:
It Is All About Perspective

by C. NaTasha Richburg

This chapter describes the stress and suffering experienced throughout Ericka's second successful IVF pregnancy. The complications experienced, coupled with the consequences of life, such as friends moving out of her life or others partaking in the envious stares of onlookers at her supportive family unit. Trying to remain in close contact with people who view our circumstances as an example of what they wished were their life, yet sharing whispers of unpleasant comments about our lives, we hear you. Telling this story is essential to giving whole meaning to our lives and their challenges.

When speaking to a group of undergraduate students exhausted from the education process, I (Ericka's mother) asked, "How many of you plan to attend graduate school?" No one raised their hand. Next, I said, "How many of you plan to live for the next five years?" Everyone raised their hands. "If you plan to live for the next five years, can you take one class each semester? If you decide to do that, you will have a graduate degree. How many of you would consider attending graduate school?" Most of them raised their hand. *It is all about perspective*, which is the mantra of our life.

We wondered why God had given us the ability to make it through times so challenging that we can't tell it all. When trying to find a more meaningful way to describe our level of stick-to-it-ness, I came across the work of Viktor Frankl. In the nih.gov article "Foundations and Applications of Logotherapy to Improve Mental Health of Immigrant Populations in the Third Millennium," Shirin Rahgozar and Lydia Giménez-Llort share, "Logotherapy is [described as] a meaning-based, value-centered psychiatric therapy developed from the works of Viktor Frankl in the early 2000s. He based logotherapy on the principle that the main motivational force of human beings is to find purpose or meaning in life." Our family has learned to find meaning in every trial. Our trials offered lessons. So, we accepted the best lesson from every circumstance. For example, a few of our lessons are:

- **Thirty-two weeks pregnant** and counting created stresses that only a belief system of empowerment could elevate the depth of the problem into the height of possibilities. In other words, we went from doctors rushing into Ericka's hospital room as the alarms of the equipment rang out; stopping to brief her on the worst-case scenario; and asking her to sign the paperwork supporting emergency surgery. The staff wondered what was different about us that prevented us from falling out in despair in the midst of crisis. We stood firm in the truth that what doesn't kill us will make us stronger.

- **The depth of the crisis** was such that we could not tell anyone because they would stress in a grasp of "Oh my God!! I will pray for you!!" at the crescendo volume that expressed fear for us. However, we would remain calm and pleasant to the hospital doctors and staff. We learned to keep some things private. We tell only those who can handle the realness of our circumstances.

- **When people believe you are privileged** because of family support, they sometimes find it challenging to celebrate you because your life's circumstances make them feel bad. Those people should no longer share in spaces with you that are deemed peaceful.

....

During many of our most urgent and dangerous hospital visits, we learned to smile and make others feel at ease as we sat prayerfully facing life-threatening peril. We want people to know how hard life is—yet uniquely satisfying at the same time. This story is an attempt to help others learn from our experiences. We hope to inspire people. We will continue to work towards our Dreams as long as we live.

10. A Smile Burns Sunlight Through Every Dark Cloud

by Ericka Michelle

"Hard is what we do" is the saying that expresses our resolve to make it through tough times. It is the ebb and flow of our life that pushes aside the fairness spoken of in fairy tales. My life was brushed in the face with reality's bristles. It became clear that motherhood would include plans to have a sibling for my child. The ideal situation included me having a committed, loving partner seeking to have a family to love and cherish. The dating scene did not yield such a person for me. Dating produced my acquaintance with a group of men who wanted me to care for them, yet keep their personal lives separate from mine. Oh yeah, they played that excellent guy role before my parents. None of them could continue hiding behind the good guy's fake face for over sixty days.

This phase of life's journey is sprinkled with the notion, "When you know better, do better." My marriage and dating history taught me the signs to look for when someone is not committed to a relation-ship with me. I am grateful to be able to move on quickly, which means my age, thirty-five, influenced my IVF journey. Older women have a greater potential for pregnancy complications. I had to move forward with an "anonymous" sperm donor for my second child, so I did not rush into a relationship. My children would be two and a half years apart, close enough to have each other as playmates. My next committed-loving relationship will be with a man who likes me, loves my children and me, and desires to be part of our collective family unit. He will come home to us nightly and not talk funny when others enter the room. He will publicly recognize me to everyone he meets as his lady. Unfortunately, time waits for no one. The biology associated with pregnancy doesn't have time to wait until the perfect man is ready to commit to a family relationship with me and my children.

This pregnancy garnered great concern from the doctors and required bed rest and constant monitoring. However, I have made it my business to be a bright light to everyone I meet in the hospital. My circumstances have never dimmed my smile. Outside of my parents and best friend, who have supported my motherhood journey, only a limited group of people checked in with me to learn the severity of our situation. Since no one checked on us (my daughter and me), we could spend our energy as the best patient for the doctors, nurses, and staff. In other words, our phones were dark during our many hospitals stays. We never suffered disappointment because of those who failed to check in. The bright light about that situation is we only had to explain our emergency hospital stays to outsiders after the fact. God knows that real-time explanations would have been challenging. We lived by the premise, *"A smile burns its sunlight through every dark cloud."*

> **"You know you are over the disappointment when you don't wish the past was different."**
>
> —Oprah Winfrey

11. The Aha Moment

by Ericka Michelle

I began the dating process after my divorce. The first person I met was lovely at first, though going through past hurts that caused him to not appeal to how I wanted to be dealt with by a man. I continued the dating process as documented in my first book, *Abandoned Guilt and Absorbed Gladness.* I was not gentle with the first guy I dated. He was my friend, and I did not protect his feelings when I moved on from him. In hindsight, I realized he was hurt though I didn't understand how then. We went our separate ways, with the friendship dissolved in the vapor of experiences not to be discussed. My family understood the young man's dilemma and said, in time, he would heal, and they wished I would get to know that version of the man.

Not considering what the family thought, I continued, meeting a series of selfish, not well-intentioned men who disappointed one after another. It only took time before I learned to identify a no-good man. One man, in particular, presented himself as a good person, pulled me in, then ghosted me. At that point, I realized that I owed my friend, my first date, an apology because he had always been the most well-intentioned and kind man I had met during my dating process. I called him to apologize. He accepted and realized through his dating process that things about his behavior could be considered off-putting. We decided to rekindle our friendship. The year-long process took on the principle of what it takes to be a friend.

My friend supported me throughout my IVF pregnancy and birth. He penned poetic expressions of a complete appreciation for our friendship. I have also presented cards and sentimental writings demonstrating how he values our friendship. Once my son was born, my friend chose not to verbalize a future picture of us as a relationship. We have since moved on only to see one another if fate directs our paths to cross.